# It's in the Bag
## Creative Thinking for School and Home

Karen S. Meador, Ph.D.

Illustrated by Christopher M. Herrin

© 1999 Pieces of Learning

pol@dnaco.net
www.piecesoflearning.com
CLC0232
ISBN 1-880505-48-7
Printed in the U.S.A.

# Dedication

For My Parents, Bliss and Martha Wilson

When I was a little girl, I had many dolls ranging from my Tiny Tears baby to a beautiful bride doll; yet, I never really wanted to play with them. I preferred to make their clothes, trying out different fabrics and designs. No one called me creative, but I guess that I was. My parents must have thought I was "different," but luckily they did not tell me. As I grew, I continued to enjoy creating and "making things." They always provided what I needed and just let me enjoy myself. It was a wonderful way to grow up!

# Table of Contents

# Activities In the Bag

# WHAT is This Activity Book About?

## Introduction

This book details the many uses of Creativity Bags. Options are suggested for monitoring them and extensions are described for Learning Center development. Each Bag activity lists materials and supplies to place in the Bag, states directions for activities on the Direction Card that is placed in the Bag, and suggests optional activities when appropriate. Use the artwork to decorate the outside of the Bag.

The take-home activities were originally designed and used in a classroom lending library for parents; however, they also have many other uses within the classroom. The creative activities utilize students' divergent thinking skills and provide an avenue for parents and educators to work with children on projects that have no "right" answers. Some activities encourage children to use critical thinking skills that require convergent thinking.

## Glossary with Examples

### Divergence

We use divergent thinking when searching for many different answers to a question or solutions to a problem. It is appropriate when there is no "right" answer or problem solution and is important when we explore possibilities.

Example: Let's think of different ways that we can get to the playground at the park.
The following ideas might result from divergent thinking:

- ride in a car   • ride on a bus   • ride bicycles   • ride motorcycles   • walk
- roller blade   • skateboard   • ride a horse   • walk on stilts

### Convergence

We use convergent thinking when searching for the single or a limited number of right answers. It is especially important when we make decisions.

Example: How did we get to the playground at the park last week?
There is only one possible answer; we rode our bikes.

### Fluency

Fluent thinking results in the production of many answers of possibilities. It is easy to recognize fluent thinkers when groups are trying to generate ideas. The fluent thinker continues to add ideas when others can think of nothing else.

Example: How can we get to the playground at the park?
The person who thinks of more and more ways to get to the playground thinks fluently.

### Flexibility

Flexible thinking helps us look at things from various perspectives. For example, in trying to determine the best way to present a new idea to someone, it is often helpful to think about it from his/ her perspective. What would the person like about the idea? Flexible thinking also helps us think of ideas and problem solutions from a variety of categories.

Example: Let's think of different ways that we can get to the playground at the park.
- Ride: car, horse, bicycles, and motorcycle   • Walk: on foot or on stilts
- Skate: skateboard or rollerblade   • Fly: airplane or hang glide   • Other: wagon

## Originality

We say that a unique idea or product is original. A person's original thinking presents something new that is not a copy.

Example: How will we get to the playground at the park today?
We can make a giant skateboard that will hold two people by putting two skateboards together with a piece of wood between them. A child can sit on the wood while an adult guides the skateboard.

## Elaboration

Elaboration takes place when we embelish ideas by adding details to a plan. Writers elaborate upon the basic elements of a story, making it more interesting and enjoyable. When we elaborate upon a basic idea the potential for using it becomes clear.

Example: How will we get to the playground at the park today?
We will ride our bikes to the park. Since the baby is too small to ride a bike, we will attach the bicycle wagon to Dad's big bike, and she can ride in it. Mom will ride the other big bike, and seven. year-old Jason will ride the small bike. We will ride on the back streets in order to avoid heavy traffic.

## Brainstorm

When brainstorming, we try to think of as many ideas as possible. We do not criticize anyone's answers, or our own; hitchhike on some of the ideas by adding to them; and accept wild and crazy ideas because they may have value.

Example: Let's brainstorm ways we could get to the playground at the park today.
• on our bikes     • in a car     • on a donkey     • on a horse
• in a cart pulled by a horse     • hang on to a bird     • put on wings and fly

## Analysis

Analysis involves taking things apart for a closer look. We may compare one thing to another, discuss the benefits or the negatives of an idea, etc. Skills of analysis help us to make informed decisions.

Example: Let's analyze whether it is safer to ride our bikes to the park or to skateboard.

## Critical Thinking and Logical Thinking

Among other things, critical thinking helps us determine whether or not information is accurate and reliable. When we think critically about decisions and choices, we base them on solid, logical reasoning. Analysis is a part of critical thinking.

## Creative Thinking

Creative thinking results in the production of ideas that are both novel and appropriate. Some of the components of creative thinking include fluency, flexibility, originality and elaboration. We use both divergent and convergent thinking in creativity.

# WHO is This Book For?

## Audience

The activities are appropriate for children in kindergarten, first grade, or second grade. Yet, it is probable that able preschoolers given adequate adult input and older children will also enjoy them.

Adults in the following roles are encouraged to use these activities:

• parents and grandparents
• primary teachers
• resource teachers
• teachers of gifted children
• librarians
• adults involved with home-schooling
• after-school care-givers

*Note: Teachers and librarians: When preparing the Bags for students to check out, provide a large student response envelope for the students' responses to the activities.

# WHY Should We Experience These Activities?

Adults have a profound effect on children who learn through observation. Spending time near an early childhood housekeeping center and watching children reenact adult scenes from their own homes confirms this effect. Children begin to form their own attitudes toward life while listening to adult conversations.

Adults encourage children to believe in the importance of critical and creative thinking when they work with youngsters on divergent activities such as those in this book.

# Educational and Life Long Learning Objectives

• To practice flexible thinking
• To generate questions
• To elaborate
• To be original
• To solve problems
• To practice critical thinking
• To forecast
• To practice logical thinking

• To analyze
• To brainstorm/practice fluency
• To recognize and express feelings
• To think divergently
• To practice creative thinking
• To practice research skills
• To understand cause and effect

# HOW Can We Use This Book?

The activities guide all adults to encourage children to use both critical and creative thinking and to help youngsters gain confidence in their ability to solve problems. The Bags meet more specific objectives for individuals in different roles.

**Parents, grandparents, and other caring adults** who treasure time spent with children enjoy having a planned activity for their quality time. Since the activities are open-ended with no right answers, adults participate on their own level and children benefit from seeing them involved in divergent thinking. Activity participants easily find humor in joint efforts and may see each other from a new perspective.

**Educators,** including primary, resource, gifted, other teachers, and librarians who use this book to create a lending "library," encourage the efforts of parents by providing them with planned activities.

**Teachers** can use the Bags in the classroom or library during the school day in a variety of ways and as activities in buddy programs and home-school settings during which older students work with younger ones. An added benefit is that the older students learn while encouraging their buddies to think in new ways.

Other classroom uses for the activities include the following:
- an assignment such as completing one Bag each week
- folder games
- center activities
- partner activities
- whole group lessons

The activities provide those who **home-school** with a planned critical and creative thinking curriculum. One student may work independently with the activities while another receives individual attention. The activities also promote interaction when children from more than one home school setting meet together.

**Librarians** can create centers with the activities and include numerous books and resource suggestions that complement the tasks. For example, children's books about emotions complement the activity titled "Feelings Are OK."

**After school care workers** and other care-givers also enjoy engaging children in the divergent thinking experiences. They can use the activities in a variety of the ways mentioned above based upon their particular environment and the number of children in their care.

# WHERE? WHEN?

Use activities from It's in the Bag at home, school, waiting at the doctor's office, airport, or a sibling's ball game, or in the car on a trip. The amount of space and materials required for each activity help determine where to complete it. While the adult and child simply talk during some activities, others utilize drawing utensils and other things that are inappropriate or unavailable in certain places.

Work with the activities when both the child and the adult are willing. Cranky children and overly-tired adults do not mix well when trying to exercise creative thinking. Both the child and the adult must feel free to express unique ideas. Allow enough time to devote to the activities so that no one feels rushed or pressured. These activities are not mandatory homework and the benefits of them result from cooperation and enjoyment.

# Managing the Activities

Busy educators find it helpful to organize and keep a record of student activities. The table below is appropriate for educators who provide the Bags for check out to students and/or parents. Write the check-out date in the cell under the child's name beside the title of the Bag; cross out the date when the Bag is returned. If you use the activities as Centers you can use the table to keep track of each student's participation. Simply put a check or note the date under the child's name by the completed Center. Although records may indicate that a student has completed a Center, be flexible and allow multiple visits until the student is satisfied with his or her learning and product.

| BAGS / STUDENTS | | | | | | | | | | |
|---|---|---|---|---|---|---|---|---|---|---|
| 1. Name the Group | | | | | | | | | | |
| 2. Strangely New | | | | | | | | | | |
| 3. What are your Questions? | | | | | | | | | | |
| 4. How Do You Feel? | | | | | | | | | | |
| 5. Feelings are OK | | | | | | | | | | |
| 6. The Problem Is... | | | | | | | | | | |
| 7. Other Uses | | | | | | | | | | |
| 8. Squeeze That Dough | | | | | | | | | | |
| 9. What Can You Do? | | | | | | | | | | |
| 10. Wish Upon a Shoe | | | | | | | | | | |
| 11. Treasure Chests | | | | | | | | | | |
| 12. Chain of Events | | | | | | | | | | |
| 13. In the Barnyard | | | | | | | | | | |
| 14. What Did You Say | | | | | | | | | | |
| 15. The Laugh That Lasted | | | | | | | | | | |

# Evaluation - Looking For Success
## Results to Expect From Divergent Thinking Activities

The activities are not a panacea for shortages of divergent thinking in the home or classroom. Yet, when used in a relaxed, risk-free environment, they offer opportunities toward understanding the importance of thinking in different ways. Some students will like certain activities more than others and may want to repeat these while omitting others that do not interest them. The impact of It's in the Bag will be greater when parents and educators honor student choice.

While all students cannot be expected to benefit from every activity, look for the following results when students enjoy having multiple experiences with the materials:
Students may . . . understand there is more than one possible answer to a question
- begin developing problem-solving skills
- benefit from working closely with an adult or older sibling
- realize they can create different types of products when completing an assignment
- learn to express their own ideas
- gain confidence in themselves through the development of answers and products that have no "right" answer
- gain personal satisfaction that may be internally motivating
- value uniqueness (It's OK to be different!)

Parents and educators also reap some of the following benefits from working with or observing children involved in the activities:
They may . . . benefit from establishing a rapport for working with the child on a school activity before it is necessary to work with him or her on a skill based or remedial assignment
- gain a clearer understanding of divergent thinking
- see new strengths or areas that require development in the child (these include both abilities in divergent thinking and creativity and personal factors such as willingness to try something different)
- see new potential for developing various types of student thinking through education and home activities
- recognize that creativity relates to a type of thinking used in more than the arts
- enjoy and value the child's ideas
- learn to honor the child's uniqueness

It's In the Bag is a beginning. We might view it as the pea under the mattress of the princess in the folk tale, The Princess and the Pea. Finding the pea was the beginning of her recognition as a princess who could marry the young prince. The activities in this book encourage children and adults to acknowledge and practice creativity; yet, this encouragement must not end with these final pages. Divergent thinking will thrive only if attitudes and actions practiced with these activities continue. Ask questions that have more than one answer, share unique thoughts and ideas with children, and honor divergence in their product development. Develop your own creative prince or princess for the vastness of a child's future kingdom is yet unknown. Looking for the pea . . . It's In the Bag!

# Name The Group

## Objective

The child will practice **flexible thinking** by noticing various characteristics of objects in pictures and using these for **categorization.**

## Bag Materials

1. Sets of pictures provided (Place Set A in one envelope and Set B in another to avoid mixing the pictures.)
2. Direction Card
3. Blank Group Names Form

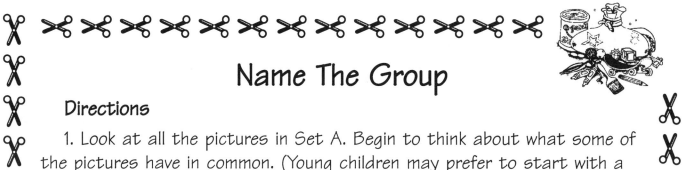

## Name The Group

### Directions

1. Look at all the pictures in Set A. Begin to think about what some of the pictures have in common. (Young children may prefer to start with a small number of pictures randomly selected from Set A.)

2. Sort the pictures into three different groups and talk about why the things in each group fit together.

### HINT

If three groups seem to frustrate the child, try putting the pictures into four or more groups first.

Remember, there are no wrong answers in Name The Group as long as you can explain why an object is in a particular group. The idea is to look at the objects in the pictures in various ways and practice flexible thinking.

3. Record the names of your groups on the Group Names Form.

### Optional

Try to form different numbers of groups. Two groups may be the hardest.

### HINT

The important part of this activity is to allow the child to think about the pictured items in more than one way. For example, a bicycle might fit in a group of things with wheels or in the transportation group.

## Modifications and/or Extensions for Centers

1. Substitute another set of pictures of objects for those provided. Adults may want to use pictures cut from magazines. Other sources include coloring books, clip-art books, and computer graphics.

2. Help the child reverse his/her thought processes by creating groups based on specified characteristics of the objects. Choices include the following:

    group by **function** (What can the objects do?)

    group by **appropriateness** of objects for three age groups such as preschoolers, middle school children, and/or adults (Who would use the objects?)

    group by **size or weight** (What size are the real objects these pictures represent?)

3. Think about how the pictures in Set B can be grouped to go with the rhymes below.

### HINT

Some are a bit tricky so encourage the child to think beyond the words of the poem and consider the situation in each.

## Mary Had a Little Lamb

| | |
|---|---|
| Mary had a little lamb, | It followed her to school one day |
| little lamb, little lamb | school one day, school one day |
| Mary had a little lamb | It followed her to school one day |
| Its fleece was white as snow. | which was against the rules. |

## Jack Sprat

| | |
|---|---|
| Jack Sprat could eat no fat | And so, betwix the two of them |
| His wife could eat no lean | They licked the platter clean. |

## Humpty Dumpty

| | |
|---|---|
| Humpty Dumpty sat on a wall. | All the king's horses |
| Humpty Dumpty had a great fall. | and all the king's men |

Couldn't put Humpty together again!

4. Choose community helpers; locate pictures of things they use; then, have the child group the items according to what goes with each helper.

# Group Names

I sorted the pictures into three groups and gave each group a name.

My groups are . . .

1. _____

2. _____

3. _____

Paste one group below. List what the objects have in common.

# Set A

# Set A (2nd page)

# Set B

# Set B (2nd page)

# Strangely New

**Objective**

The child will use **flexible thinking** and **analysis** to explore purposeful possibilities.

**Bag Materials**

1. Pictures of animals provided
2. Directions Card
3. Paper for drawing
4. Optional: crayons, markers, and/or pencils

## Strangely New

### Directions

1. Choose two of the animals from the pictures provided.

2. Discuss the similarities and differences between the animals.

3. Discuss the function or purpose of some of the characteristics or attributes of each animal. For example, how does the trunk help an elephant?

4. Choose at least two characteristics from the animal in one picture and think about how these might look if they were placed on the other animal.

5. Draw a picture of the "new" animal or object. For example, when thinking about a frog and a porcupine, you might borrow the porcupine quills and place them on the frog.

6. Discuss the abilities or functions of the "new" animal. What can it do now that it could not do before the change? For example, the frog with porcupine quills could now protect itself by poking things with the quills.

### Optional

Complete the activity using two other animals.

Work with four animals discussing similarities and differences among the four. Apply some of the characteristics of three of the animals to the fourth one.

### HINT

It is important for the child to talk about how adding characteristics helps to change functions or abilities. This lays a foundation for understanding that **innovation** often results from **combining things in a new way.**

## Extensions and/or Modifications for Centers

1. When discussing similarities and differences, the difficulty level can be raised by using an animal and an inanimate object that have few, if any, similarities. When there are few physical similarities, children must consider functions and abstract characteristics.

For example, a dog and horse have obvious physical similarities such as eyes, tails, and ears. A dog and a motorcycle, however, do not look alike, so the child must consider other similarities such as noting they can both "go fast," "belong to someone," and/or "help you have fun." An adult may need to ask probing questions such as the following:

Is there anything they can both do?

Would we ever find both things in the same place?

Is there anything a person could do to both of them?

2. Create a matching game using the pictures of unusual animals and the original animals. The child matches each newly created animal with the animal(s) from which its new characteristics were borrowed.

### Note

This is a **convergent thinking** task. It does, however, prepare the child to understand the potential for **innovation** through combining of what already exists.

18

# What Are Your Questions?

### Objective

The child will practice *generating questions* in order to gather information and *elaborate* upon a visual cue.

### Bag Materials

1. Interesting illustrations (Choose from the illustrations provided or select from other sources such as children's books.)
2. Direction Card
3. <u>Questions Sheet</u>
4. School Project - Envelope for completed questions

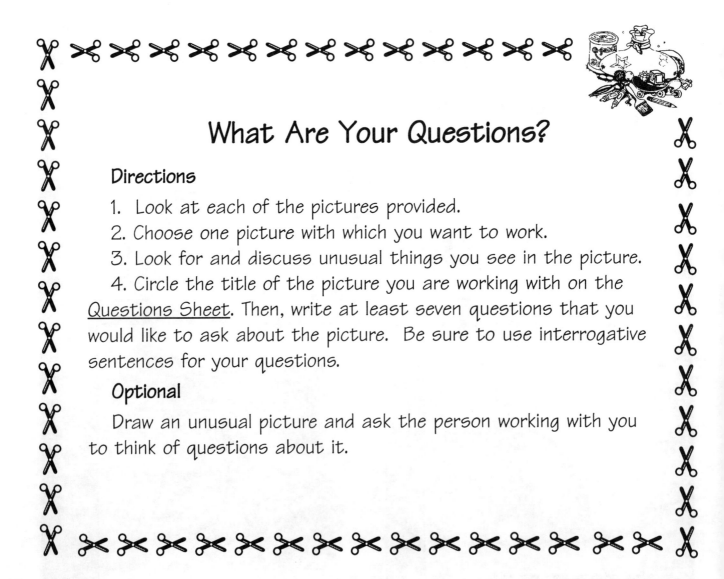

## What Are Your Questions?

### Directions

1. Look at each of the pictures provided.
2. Choose one picture with which you want to work.
3. Look for and discuss unusual things you see in the picture.
4. Circle the title of the picture you are working with on the <u>Questions Sheet</u>. Then, write at least seven questions that you would like to ask about the picture. Be sure to use interrogative sentences for your questions.

### Optional

Draw an unusual picture and ask the person working with you to think of questions about it.

## Modifications and/or Extensions for Centers

Ask the child to create a picture in which some things look a little unusual. Provide magazines from which the child can select and cut parts to make the picture. The picture might contain a boy walking in a winter coat while other children play nearby in summer clothing. Encourage another child to ask questions about the picture.

## HINT

The cut and paste method mentioned above is a quick way for adults to create new pictures to use in the original activity. Consider adding a figure from a comic strip to a picture from a magazine or other source.

today's class:
STICK SOUP

**23**

# Questions Sheet

### Circle the name of the picture you are using.

Cooking Class          Swimmer          Skateboarding Gorilla          Frogs in the Rain

1. _____

2. _____

3. _____

4. _____

5. _____

6. _____

7. _____

# How Do You Feel?

## Objective

The child will develop an **awareness of emotions** and their descriptive vocabulary in order to be more expressive regarding personal feelings.

## Bag Materials

1. Illustrations
2. Scissors, glue, manila paper, pencils
3. Direction Card
4. Optional: A children's book about feelings.

## How Do You Feel?

### Directions

1. **Optional** Read a book about feelings, if available.

2. Make a list of words that stand for feelings. This may include glad, happy, miserable, joyful, sad, disgusted.

### HINT

Many children have limited vocabulary regarding emotions; therefore, feel free to offer additional words.

3. Discuss the illustrations and talk about what might have happened to cause them to display emotions. Talk about and name a feeling indicated by each figure. It may help to look at the list of words created in #2.

4. Discuss a time when you felt the emotion shown by two or three of the illustrations. What caused you to feel that way? Did your feelings change later?

5. Cut out and glue two or more of the illustrations onto paper. Below each figure, use the "feelings" word that best describes the picture in a sentence telling when you felt that way. For example, "I felt excited when I got a new puppy."

### HINT

Emotions affect the decisions people make, and it is important for children to understand their feelings and channel them positively.

**Suggested Reading**

Books That Discuss Feelings

Modesitt, J. <u>Sometimes I Feel like a Mouse: a Book about Feelings</u>. New York: Scholastic. 1992.
  This short book has large print and good illustrations depicting a child feeling shy, excited, scared, ashamed, proud, etc.

Palmer, P. <u>I Wish I Could Hold Your Hand . . . a Child's Guide to Grief and Loss</u>. San Luis Obispo CA: Impact Publishers. 1994.
  Dr. Palmer speaks gently to children through this black and white book. He discusses normal emotions and suggests that "it is a good thing to let yourself feel . . ." (p. 26).

Books That Depict or Elicit Emotion

Harris, W. <u>Judy and the Volcano</u>. New York: Scholastic. 1994.
  This selection is about Judy whose teacher, Mrs. Be-the-best-you-can, wants her to write a story. Judy's vivid facial expressions provide ample opportunities to discuss the feelings behind her looks.

Henkes, K. <u>Lilly's Purple Plastic Purse</u>. New York: Greenwillow Books. 1996.
  Lilly displays a variety of feelings arising from annoying her teacher with her new purse and its jingling contents.

Kilborne, S. <u>Peach & Blue</u>. New York: Alfred A. Knopf. 1994.
  Emotions are obvious in illustrations of this charming story of a frog named Blue who helps Peach explore her surroundings.

**Extensions and/or Modifications for Centers**

1. Provide books about feelings for the child to read. Tape record these for nonreaders.
2. Allow the child to help make a **Word Wall** by writing the words that describe feelings on paper rectangles and randomly attaching them to the wall.
3. Tape record short portions of different types of music and ask the child to tell or write how the music makes them feel.
4. Provide 6 inch squares of paper and ask the child to use paint or color to represent various feelings. Suggest the use of color without drawing a picture. These may be pieced together to form a class "feelings" quilt. Use the colored pieces alternately with plain white squares. Words may be written on the white squares if desired. A child may create an individual quilt using small squares of paper.

# Feelings Are OK

**Objective**

The child will notice that *feelings are important* and should be recognized.

**Bag Materials**

1. A copy of the short written episode, "The Play."
2. Direction Card
3. Response paper

Note: It will be helpful to complete <u>How Do You Feel?</u> prior to the following activity.

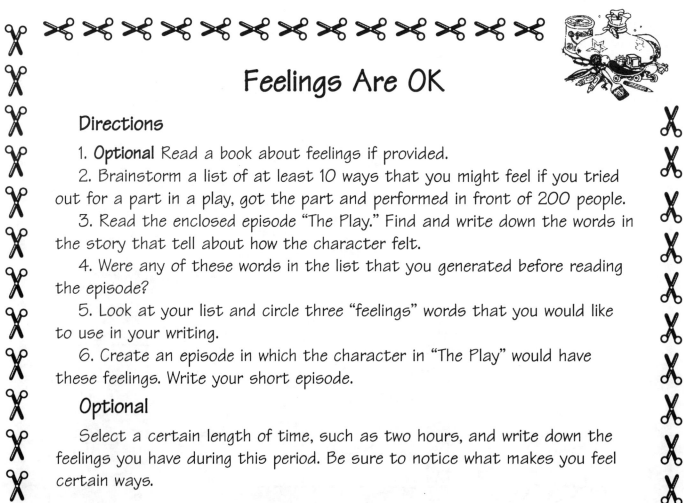

## Feelings Are OK

### Directions

1. **Optional** Read a book about feelings if provided.

2. Brainstorm a list of at least 10 ways that you might feel if you tried out for a part in a play, got the part and performed in front of 200 people.

3. Read the enclosed episode "The Play." Find and write down the words in the story that tell about how the character felt.

4. Were any of these words in the list that you generated before reading the episode?

5. Look at your list and circle three "feelings" words that you would like to use in your writing.

6. Create an episode in which the character in "The Play" would have these feelings. Write your short episode.

### Optional

Select a certain length of time, such as two hours, and write down the feelings you have during this period. Be sure to notice what makes you feel certain ways.

# The Play

The teacher said that her class was going to perform a short play at the next parent-teacher meeting. Everyone in the class would be in the play, and those students who had speaking parts would need to memorize their lines. Josh felt very worried when he heard this because he did not know whether he could remember what to say.

The teacher also talked about the costumes for the play and said that the boy who played the part of the prince would wear a jeweled crown. Josh was happy when he thought about how proud he would be if he got to wear a crown.

There would be tryouts for the speaking parts on Wednesday after school, so the teacher sent a note home about this. Josh worried about whether or not to give the note to his mom. He knew that she would want him to try for a speaking part; but he was concerned about whether he could do it. Finally, after encouragement from Mom, Josh decided to "go for it." He was very excited on the day of the tryouts.

Josh thought school would never end on Wednesday, and he watched the clock all the time. Part of the day he felt ecstatic about how neat it would be to get a part; however, the rest of the day he felt depressed thinking about how he would feel if he did not get a part. Finally, the school bell rang, and it was time for tryouts.

**Extensions and/or Modifications for Centers**

1. Provide "play starters," short beginnings of plays that the child may choose to complete if not using an original idea. Two are provided; however, these are more meaningful if composed specifically for the child or children completing the activity.

2. Make available books about emotions so that the child establishes a "feelings" vocabulary.

3. Let each student make his or her own dictionary of words that describe feelings. Books for this are easily made by placing three or more sheets of white paper on top of a piece of colored paper. Use a sewing machine to stitch down the center of these in order to connect the pages and make the crease. Fold the paper in half on the stitching. Students may copy words from the books they read, from index cards prepared by an adult, or from other sources.

## Play Starter #1

| Characters | Ben, an eight-year-old boy who has two sisters |
|---|---|
| | Jan, Ben's four-year-old sister |
| | Joan, Ben's six-year-old sister who plays the piano |
| Setting | Ben's shaded back yard in a small town in the middle of a hot summer and inside Ben's house |

"Feelings" Words to use: disgusted and alarmed

"That does it!" said Ben, slamming the door as he angrily marched into the back yard. "Why do I have to listen to that kid banging on the piano when I want to watch cartoons on television?" Ben was talking about Joan, his six year old sister who . . .

## Play Starter #2

| Characters | Mr. Jordan, who owns a grocery store |
|---|---|
| | Mrs. Smith, a school teacher with three children of her own |
| | Sam, Mrs. Smith's three-year-old son |
| | Mrs. James, a woman whose children are grown |
| Setting | Mr. Jordan's grocery store in the middle of a busy Saturday |

"Feelings" Words to use: concerned and pleased

Sam loved to go to the grocery store with his mom. There were always interesting things to look at, and at age three he was proud to be big enough to walk around the store instead of having to sit in the grocery basket. Now Sam could get his hands on things and really enjoy himself.

# Squeeze That Dough

**Objective**

The child will understand the meaning of *originality.*

**Bag Materials**

1. A batch of homemade playdough
2. Playdough recipe
3. Direction Card
4. Drawing paper

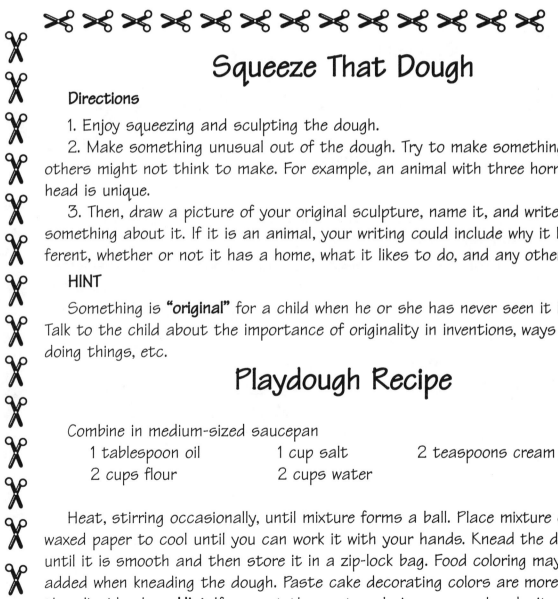

## Squeeze That Dough

### Directions

1. Enjoy squeezing and sculpting the dough.

2. Make something unusual out of the dough. Try to make something that others might not think to make. For example, an animal with three horns on its head is unique.

3. Then, draw a picture of your original sculpture, name it, and write something about it. If it is an animal, your writing could include why it looks different, whether or not it has a home, what it likes to do, and any other ideas.

### HINT

Something is **"original"** for a child when he or she has never seen it before. Talk to the child about the importance of originality in inventions, ways of doing things, etc.

## Playdough Recipe

Combine in medium-sized saucepan

| 1 tablespoon oil | 1 cup salt | 2 teaspoons cream of tartar |
| 2 cups flour | 2 cups water | |

Heat, stirring occasionally, until mixture forms a ball. Place mixture on waxed paper to cool until you can work it with your hands. Knead the dough until it is smooth and then store it in a zip-lock bag. Food coloring may be added when kneading the dough. Paste cake decorating colors are more vivid than liquid colors. **Hint** If you get the paste coloring on your hands, it can be removed with toothpaste.

# The Problem Is . . .

**Objective**

The child will think *divergently* about how common objects can be combined to help solve a problem.

**Bag Materials**

1. An assortment of objects (example: a ruler, an empty coffee can, a pencil, string, etc.)
2. Optional: A Pig Tale or another book with a similar theme. A Pig Tale by Olivia Newton-John (1993, New York: Simon & Schuster Books for Young Readers) depicts Ziggy's pop who collected things and turned them into "an amazing invention."
3. "The Problem Is . . ." selections
4. Direction Card
5. Inventor's Worksheet (see page 41)

## The Problem Is . . .

### Directions

1. **Optional** Read A Pig Tale by Olivia Newton-John if available or another book about inventing.

2. Read **"The Problem Is . . ."** selections and choose one of these with which to work.

3. Use the objects provided or other things you have at home to create an invention that would help solve the problem given in your selection. You do not have to use all the objects.

4. Draw a picture of your invention on the Inventor's Worksheet provided. Explain your invention and tell what problem it solves. Now, write your explanation on the worksheet.

### Extension

Make a list of problems at your home or at school that new inventions might solve.

### HINT

Please allow the child to exaggerate the properties of objects when creating the invention.

34

© Pieces of Learning CLC0232

# "The Problem Is . . . "

Kim has a cat named Mrs. Robinson who likes to play with cat toys.
**The problem is** that Mrs. Robinson loses her toys. They get stuck behind heavy furniture, left outdoors, and all kinds of things. Kim is really tired of buying new cat things, so today she wants to make a toy. Please help her make something interesting for Mrs. Robinson.

# "The Problem Is . . ."

When Hank goes to the grocery store, he always takes a list, since he has a pretty bad memory. **The problem is** that he misplaces the list after he gets to the store. He knows that he should keep it in his pocket, but that does not always work. He may leave the list in the apple pile, the milk cooler, or other places. What can you create to help Hank from misplacing his list?

# "The Problem Is . . ."

Aunt Jane likes to read in bed at night because it seems to make her sleepy. **The problem is** that she usually falls asleep with her book open and when it flips shut, she loses her place. She has tried using a bookmark, but cannot seem to get it in place before she falls asleep. Can you help Aunt Jane?

# "The Problem Is . . . "

Do you ever let your mind wander when you should be thinking about something important? This happens to many people. One day, while Sue's mind was on a trip, she thought of an interesting-looking piece of art she could use in her room. **The problem is** that now she does not remember what it looked like. Can you make something interesting to help remind her of the art piece she wants to make?

# "The Problem Is . . . "

When Jerry rides his bike to school, he knows he will have a problem getting ready to go home. **The problem is** there are four other bikes just like Jerry's that belong to other kids. So, Jerry has a hard time knowing which bike to ride home. He does not want to write his name on his bike. He wants something cool! Make something to help Jerry.

# "The Problem Is . . ."

Harry hamster, who lives in Mr. James' first grade classroom, enjoys looking at new and different things that the children put just outside his cage. He has looked in a mirror, stared at pictures made by the children, and yearned to lie down on a pretty pillow someone brought. **The problem is** the children seem to have run out of ideas about what to show Harry. Can you make something to help?

# Inventor's Worksheet

Description of Problem Being Solved

_____

_____

_____

Materials Used for Solution

_____

_____

Explanation (Description) of Solution

_____

_____

_____

Sketch the solution below.

# Other Uses

## Objective

The child will practice *flexible thinking* by finding alternate uses for common objects. Note: This type of activity is commonly used in creativity training and assessment.

## Bag Materials

1. Direction Card
2. Paper for drawing

## Other Uses

### Directions

1. Choose one of the objects from the list below. If you want to make a random choice, close your eyes and allow your pointer finger to land on the words. Use the word closest to your finger.

| | | |
|---|---|---|
| a yardstick | a mop | a toy dump truck |
| a picture frame | a mixing bowl | a baseball |
| an empty soda can | a broken toy | an old hat |
| a sheet for a bed | a magazine after you are finished with it | |

2. Brainstorm a list of at least five (5) things for which you might use the object. Try to create unique uses that no one else would think about. It's O.K. if your ideas are a bit unusual. For example, have you ever seen a yardstick tied to a child's foot and used to practice skiing? This is an original idea used by a five-year-old.

3. Repeat step 2 with another object on the list or one found around your home. Sometimes you can think of unusual ideas by looking at the real object from various angles. Be sure to turn the object sideways and upside down.

## Modifications and/or Extensions for Centers

1. Encourage the child to think about what could be added to the selected object in order to make it more interesting when used in a new way. For example, someone added an aroma to stickers to make them more appealing. Provide samples of various textures, colors, designs, scents (on cotton balls enclosed in baby food jars), etc. to help the child generate ideas.

2. Add a different object to the activity every day or two.

3. It is fun to include pictures of different environments such as the playground, a kitchen, school room, or office to encourage the child to think of using objects in a variety of settings. Sketch your own, use children's drawings, or clip magazine pictures to use.

4. Later, the child may enjoy seeing this activity again with a slightly different twist. For example, how could the child use two objects working together?

5. Provide paper and drawing materials for recording ideas.

# What Can You Do?

## Objective

The child will practice *fluent, flexible, original,* and *elaborative thinking* by using objects and shapes in producing novel ideas.

## Bag Materials

1. Direction Card
2. Patterns of parts of a shoe: Cut-out patterns for the child to draw around during activity
3. Drawing paper
4. Crayons

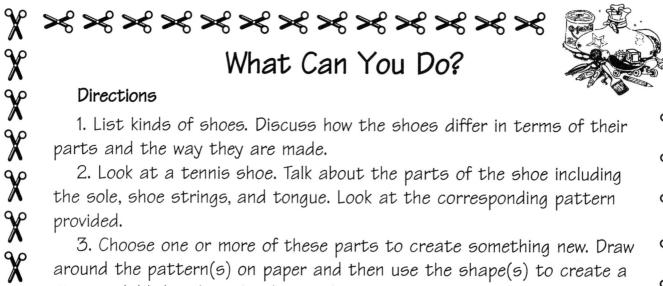

## What Can You Do?

### Directions

1. List kinds of shoes. Discuss how the shoes differ in terms of their parts and the way they are made.

2. Look at a tennis shoe. Talk about the parts of the shoe including the sole, shoe strings, and tongue. Look at the corresponding pattern provided.

3. Choose one or more of these parts to create something new. Draw around the pattern(s) on paper and then use the shape(s) to create a picture. Add detail to the drawing by putting things in and around your idea. You may work with an adult friend on one picture or each decide to make individual drawings.

4. Talk about the completed drawing(s). Why did the shape make you think of drawing this picture? Is there any way to add more detail to the picture(s)?

### HINT

This activity allows participants to exercise four major components of creative thinking: **fluency, flexibility, originality,** and **elaboration. Brainstorming** provides an opportunity for **fluent thinking, generating** as many ideas as possible without judging their quality. In step 4, **flexible thinking** helps participants see the shapes as a **variety** of different things. When drawing the picture, a unique or **original** idea may be produced and then **elaborated** upon by adding detail. If the child enjoys this activity, why not pick another object and try it again later?

# Shoe Patterns

**Extensions and/or Modifications for Centers**

1. Put a box of old shoes in the center to help stimulate ideas.

2. Invite the child to use a different type shoe for the drawing activity. The child may require aid in creating the patterns of the parts of the chosen shoe.

# Wish Upon a Shoe

## Objectives

1. The child will use **creative thinking** by considering purposeful modifications of an object.
2. The child will exercise **critical thinking** through decision-making and selection of an idea.

## Bag Materials

1. Paper
2. A pencil and crayons
3. Direction Card
4. Decision Matrix

## Wish Upon a Shoe

### Directions

1. Walk around the room or outdoors while talking about why you wear shoes. What do your shoes allow you to do that you would not want to do without them on your feet?

2. Talk about what you WISH your shoes could do for you. Would you like shoes that help you fly, walk on ice, or make you look taller? Make a list of at least five things you wish shoes helped you do. Wild and crazy ideas are appropriate!

3. Use the Decision Matrix to help decide which one idea you want to investigate.

4. Now, can you make that idea come true? What can be added to your shoes to allow you to get your wish? For example, if someone wished their shoes would help them get places faster, the person might think about adding electric-powered wheels to the shoe. Talk about what you can do to make your wish come true.

5. Draw a picture of your original super duper shoe.

### HINT

This activity helps the child learn that new products are often based upon need or desire for improvement. The Decision Matrix, while somewhat advanced for young children, helps children exercise **critical thinking** by basing a decision on criteria.

# Decision Matrix

Write your five ideas down the left column of the matrix. Rate each idea from 1-5 on the criteria provided, using 5 as the most positive. For example, if the idea would not be fun, rate it 1. You may use the same number more than once. Work with the idea that receives the highest total points. If two ideas score the same, choose your favorite.

| Ideas | Would Be Fun | Is Possible | Would Be Pretty Safe | Total |
|---|---|---|---|---|
| 1. | | | | |
| 2. | | | | |
| 3. | | | | |
| 4. | | | | |
| 5. | | | | |

**Extensions and/or Modifications for Centers**

1. Create similar follow-up activities by changing the shoe to another object. For example, a child might wish that a ball would make a noise as it rolled. Provide several different objects so the child can make choices.

2. If the child can read, include a wish list describing what others want objects to do and ask students to draw the needed invention.

Suggestions for this include:

I wish my bike played music when I rode it.
I wish my pencil would stay sharp all the time.
I wish my socks would not slip down in my shoes.
I wish my homework did not get wrinkled in my book bag.
I wish my hat could keep my body from getting wet in the rain.

3. **Option** Provide pictures of unique inventions, if available, to show possibilities. Books about inventions are also good resources.

# Treasure Chests

**Objective**

The child will practice **research skills** to help determine objects of value to specific individuals.

**Bag Materials**

1. <u>Information Guide</u>
2. Blank treasure chest picture
3. Direction Card
4. Pencil or crayons

## Treasure Chests

### Directions

1. Talk about things that you treasure such as sea shells from a vacation, a favorite picture, a trophy, or special notes from a friend. Make a list of items that you would put in a treasure chest. You may want to draw the items on the treasure chest picture provided.

2. Discuss the fact that people treasure different things, and talk about what a person who walked on the beach might treasure.

3. Select one of the jobs on the <u>Information Guide</u>. Talk about it; read the information; and discuss the types of things a person with this job might place in a treasure chest. Try to think of at least five items. These might include the tools they use or things they have found. Draw or write the names of these items on a blank treasure chest.

4. If you want, complete this activity with a different job.

### Optional

Draw a picture of someone doing a job or write some information about a person's occupation. Then prepare a treasure chest for the person.

### Optional

This activity could be completed using a character from a book. For example, what would Little Red Riding Hood have in her treasure chest?

### HINT

A child must think abstractly from another person's point of view in order to suggest what that person might treasure.

## Extensions and/or Modifications for Centers

1. Display multiple pictures of tools used for jobs and/or people involved in different jobs, sports, or hobbies, so the child will have many choices. A few of these are provided for you. Feature simple information about each character in written or tape recorded form. Consider the following suggestions:

- a cowboy
- a chef
- a scuba diver
- a game or forest warden
- a librarian
- an archeologist
- a chemist
- a professional clown
- a teacher

2. Encourage the child to draw his/her own people and find out more about them by looking in resource books.

# Information Guide

### Airline Pilot

Airline pilots, who may be men or women, spend much of their work time inside an airplane. Occasionally, they stop in interesting places, but have little time for sightseeing. They sleep in a hotel and go right back to the airport. Some pilots have special things they take with them for their overnight stays. These help remind them of their home or family. A pilot may plan a longer stay in a city or part of the world they want to explore. Often, they bring home souvenirs from these places.

### Secretary or Office Worker

People who work in an office usually spend part of their day answering the telephone, filing, using a computer, and working at a desk. They find ways to make the job easier and more pleasant by bringing things from home or buying things at an office supply store. Many secretaries and office workers put cheerful items on their desks or walls.

### Rancher

People who work on a ranch spend a lot of time outdoors. Sometimes they find interesting rocks, pieces of wood, or other things lying on the ground. Some ranchers work with cattle, so they often build and repair fences to help keep their herd where it belongs.

### House Painter

Painters always seem to have a brush in one of their pockets and paint on their clothes. Some painters wear caps on their heads to keep the paint out of their hair. They have to be careful not to fall off the ladder when painting the tops of houses. They find all sorts of interesting things, such as bird's nests, under the eaves of houses. Most painters carry a small radio to play while they work.

### Doctor

Men and women doctors use many different tools when they work. These include tongue depressors, needles, stethoscopes, and other things. Some doctors may have treats for children in their pockets. They take care of people who are ill and write prescriptions for medications to help make them well.

# My Treasure Chest

# Career Tools

# Chain of Events

## Objectives

1. The child will use **critical thinking skills** to realize that one event affects another.
2. The child will **forecast** the possible events following a particular situation.
3. The child will realize how people can **affect changes.**

## Bag Materials

1. Paper
2. Event List
3. Direction Card

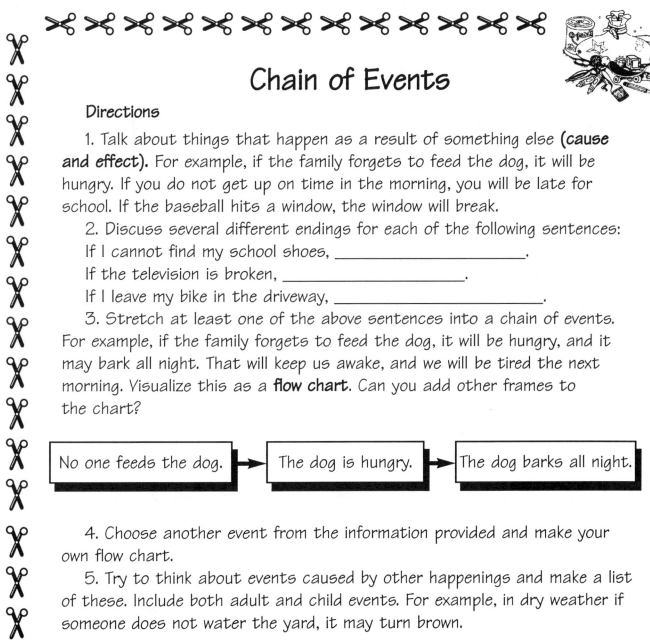

## Chain of Events

### Directions

1. Talk about things that happen as a result of something else (**cause and effect**). For example, if the family forgets to feed the dog, it will be hungry. If you do not get up on time in the morning, you will be late for school. If the baseball hits a window, the window will break.

2. Discuss several different endings for each of the following sentences:

If I cannot find my school shoes, _____.

If the television is broken, _____.

If I leave my bike in the driveway, _____.

3. Stretch at least one of the above sentences into a chain of events. For example, if the family forgets to feed the dog, it will be hungry, and it may bark all night. That will keep us awake, and we will be tired the next morning. Visualize this as a **flow chart**. Can you add other frames to the chart?

| No one feeds the dog. | → | The dog is hungry. | → | The dog barks all night. |

4. Choose another event from the information provided and make your own flow chart.

5. Try to think about events caused by other happenings and make a list of these. Include both adult and child events. For example, in dry weather if someone does not water the yard, it may turn brown.

# Event List

The doorbell rang.

The phone rang in the middle of the night.

We could not find my shoes, and it was time for school.

The kitchen floor was muddy when Mom came home from the grocery store.

The teacher gave students their report cards.

There was a mouse in the kitchen.

The teacher gave me a note to take home.

My jeans were too small.

### Extensions and/or Modifications for Centers

Provide a completed chain of events flow chart and ask the child to complete one using another event. Provide blank flow charts for the work.

### Optional

Provide objects that the child may use to arrange a physical chain reaction. For example, when a rolling ball hits a Unifix® cube or Lego® wall, the wall falls over and hits a paper cup. The child can set up larger chain reactions using other things. (Please discuss the importance of being careful to avoid breaking anything or annoying another person.)

### School Project

When using this as a center for nonreaders, pictures of occurrences may be substituted for written descriptions.

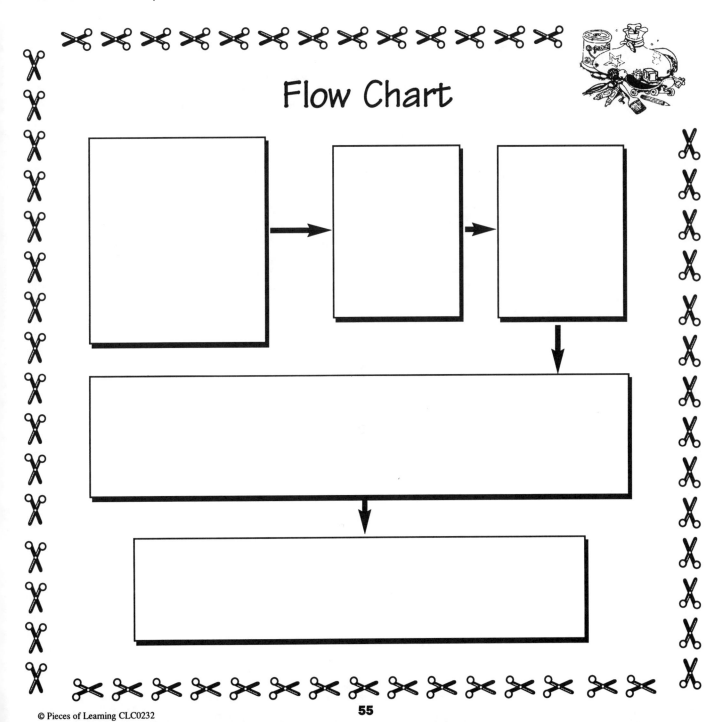

# Flow Chart

# Flow Chart

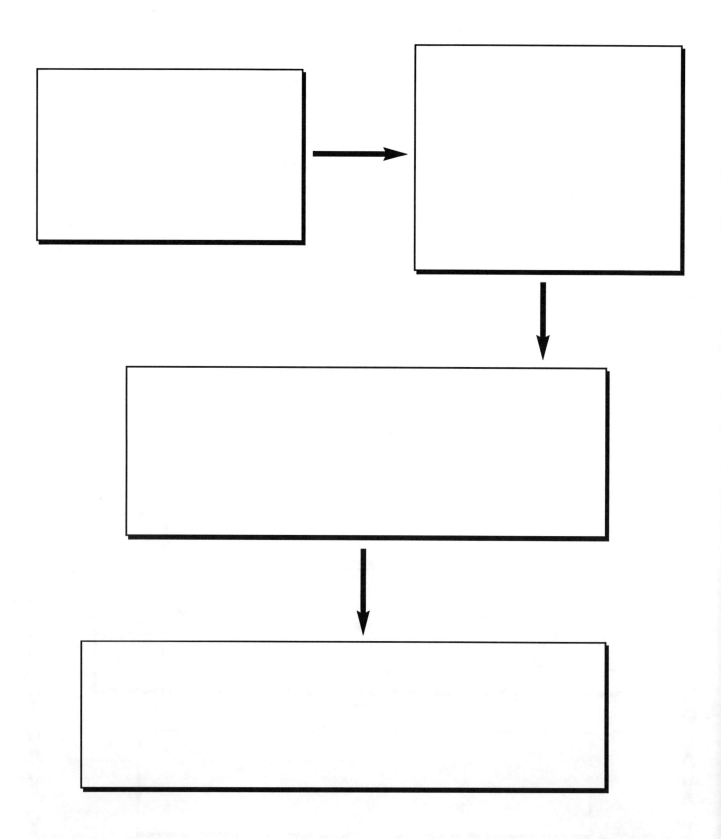

# In the Barnyard

## Objective

The child will exercise *logical thinking* by solving a problem requiring consideration of multiple options.

## Bag Materials

1. Barnyard Information
2. Direction Card
3. Paper
4. Optional: small plastic farm animals

## In the Barnyard

### Directions

1. Read Part A of the Barnyard Information.

2. Fill in one of the logic charts regarding which animals can live beside the others in the barnyard. Write yes or no in the blanks.

3. Use this information to figure out where to put the animals in the barnyard. If small animals are provided, arrange them in pen fences made with toothpicks. Then write animal names or draw pictures in their proper pens drawn on a piece of paper, as shown below.

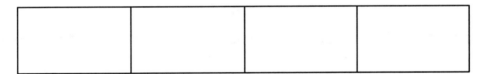

### Optional

Plan and draw a new configuration of the four pens in the barnyard. How, if at all, would this affect the pen designated for each animal? A suggested example follows:

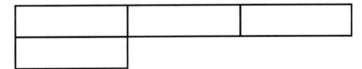

### HINT

Help the child see the value of planning ahead and considering many factors when making a decision. Ask them about times when the family has to consider the opinions, interests, and/or needs of several people before making a decision.

# Barnyard Information

## Part A

Emily Perky has cows, pigs, chickens, and horses on her farm. Every so often the animals get into trouble with each other and have to be moved to different parts of the barnyard. The barnyard is a long rectangle divided into four parts like the diagram below.

| | | | |
|---|---|---|---|
| | | | |

Last week, Emily had the following things to think about:
• The chickens go under the fence and get in the mud with the pigs.
• They get mud all over themselves and then make a big mess in the nests where they lay eggs.
• The horses try to get into the pen with the chickens. They seem to think that the chicken's food looks good and try to break down the fence to get to the chicken coop.

Use the logic chart below and then arrange the barnyard the way you think Emily did last week.

## Logic Chart
### Which of These Animals Can Live Beside the Others? (Write Yes or No)

| | Horses | Cows | Pigs | Chickens |
|---|---|---|---|---|
| **Horses** | ■ | | | |
| **Cows** | | ■ | | |
| **Pigs** | | | ■ | |
| **Chickens** | | | | ■ |

## Barnyard

| | | | |
|---|---|---|---|
| | | | |

# Barnyard Information

## Part B

Unfortunately, the first arrangement worked for two months and then the animals developed another problem. Three of the cows had calves that were frightened by the snorting of the pigs. It made the mother cows very nervous, too. If Emily used your first barnyard arrangement, would she have to move the pigs after the cows were born? If so, how would you arrange the barnyard now?

## Logic Chart
### Which of These Animals Can Live Beside the Others? (Write Yes or No)

|          | Horses | Cows | Pigs | Chickens |
|----------|--------|------|------|----------|
| Horses   |        |      |      |          |
| Cows     |        |      |      |          |
| Pigs     |        |      |      |          |
| Chickens |        |      |      |          |

## Barnyard

|   |   |   |   |
|---|---|---|---|
|   |   |   |   |

**Extensions and/or Modifications for Centers**

1. Let the child deal with more animals and other problems in the barnyard.

2. Add other elements to consider in the planning such as the barn, open pasture, etc.

3. A young child may benefit from drawing the animals, cutting them out, and creating a barnyard scene.

# What Did You Say?

**Objective**

The child will **think flexibly** in order to explore meanings of common phrases.
Note: This lesson is more appropriate for late first grade or second grade children than for those in kindergarten.

**Bag Materials**

1. Phrases (Use a minimum of four of the words, phrases, or quotes provided. Choose these appropriately according to difficulty.)
2. Drawing paper
3. Direction Card

## What Did You Say?

### Directions

1. Talk about common words or phrases used in conversation that adults seem to understand but may confuse children. These include "a baker's dozen (13)," "cat got your tongue?" and others.

2. Select several of the words or phrases provided and talk about what each means. Discuss situations in which a person might use each phrase.

3. Use your own words to write an explanation of what you think one of these words or phrases means.

4. Discuss the possible reasons people use these words or phrases. Do they make communication easier, more interesting, or more confusing?

### Optional

1. Listen for common phrases people use in your house, at school, or on television. Write these down and discuss them.

2. Draw a humorous picture to represent "river road," "moving target," "tow truck," or "fingerbowl." Let someone else guess the word(s) your picture represents.

## Extensions and/or Modifications for Centers

1. Provide other age-appropriate sayings for the child to explain. If these explanations are tape-recorded, others can enjoy listening to them later. Children also delight in listening to themselves!

2. A child may choose to provide an interpretation by drawing a picture, writing a rap, dramatizing the sayings, or using another form of expression.

## Words and Phrases

Note: These are listed in groups according to difficulty. Choose those appropriate for the child.

## Group I

Time flies when you're having fun.
Watch Dog
Bookworm
Loud Shirt
Pig-out!

## Group II

Out of sight, out of mind.
A stitch in time saves nine.
Has the cat got your tongue?
A picture is worth a thousand words.

## Group III

When fate hands us a lemon, let's try to make a lemonade.
- Dale Carnegie
Kindness begets kindness. - Sophocles
Too many cooks spoil the broth.
Know thyself. - Socrates
(Writing is) a different name for conversation.

## Group IV

He conquers who endures. - Persius
There are no degrees of honesty. - Anonymous
A library is a hospital for the mind. - Anonymous
Enthusiasm is contagious and so is the lack of it. - Anonymous

# The Laugh That Lasted

Note: The word "Tickleoctopus" comes from the book, <u>The Tickleoctopus</u> written by Audrey and Don Wood.

**Objective**

The child will use creative thinking to make a Tickleoctopus.

**Bag Materials**

The supplies for this project vary according to the type of material the child chooses for making a Tickleoctopus.

1. Direction Card
2. Scissors
3. Glue
4. Assorted Materials - construction paper, ribbon, cotton balls, feathers, etc.

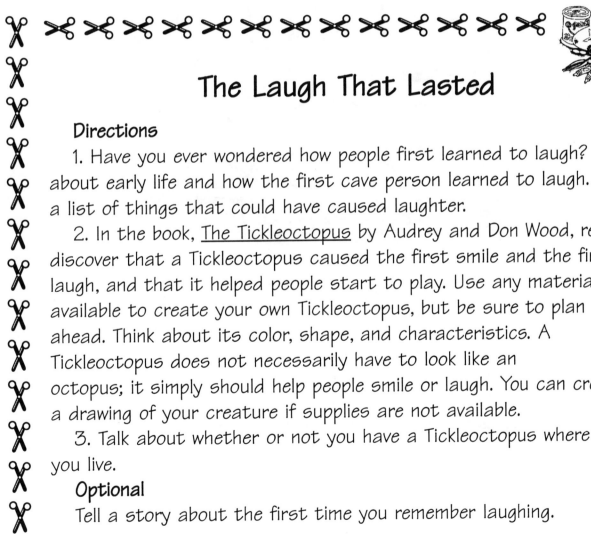

## The Laugh That Lasted

### Directions

1. Have you ever wondered how people first learned to laugh? Think about early life and how the first cave person learned to laugh. Make a list of things that could have caused laughter.

2. In the book, <u>The Tickleoctopus</u> by Audrey and Don Wood, readers discover that a Tickleoctopus caused the first smile and the first laugh, and that it helped people start to play. Use any materials available to create your own Tickleoctopus, but be sure to plan ahead. Think about its color, shape, and characteristics. A Tickleoctopus does not necessarily have to look like an octopus; it simply should help people smile or laugh. You can create a drawing of your creature if supplies are not available.

3. Talk about whether or not you have a Tickleoctopus where you live.

### Optional

Tell a story about the first time you remember laughing.

## Extensions and/or Modifications for Centers

1. Provide a copy of The Tickleoctopus for students to look at and read. Tape record the story for nonreaders.

2. Place assorted pictures in the center and ask students to pick those in which people might have been near a Tickleoctopus. Ask students to write or tape record stories about the person's encounter with a Tickleoctopus.

3. Provide play dough or clay for sculpting a Tickleoctopus.

4. Allow students to make foil covered wire models of the Tickleoctopus. Students sculpt a shape with pliable wire or sturdy pipe cleaners and then cover it with wrinkled foil. Scrap foil can be used. (It will be necessary to supervise this activity unless there is a limitless supply of foil.)

### References

Burns, M. The Greedy Triangle. New York: Scholastic Inc. 1994.

Deedy, C. The Library Dragon. New York: Scholastic Inc. 1994.

Deedy, C. Tree Man. Atlanta, GA: Peachtree Publishers, Ltd. 1993.

Harris, W. Judy and the Volcano. New York: Scholastic. 1994.

Henkes, K. Lilly's Purple Plastic Purse. New York: Greenwillow Books. 1996.

Kilborne, S. Peach & Blue. New York: Alfred A. Knopf. 1994.

Lincoln, W. and Suid, M. The Teacher's Quotation Book. Palo Alto, CA: Dale Seymour Publications. 1986.

Modesitt, J. Sometimes I Feel like a Mouse: a Book about Feelings. New York: Scholastic. 1992.

Newton-John, O. A Pig Tale. New York: Simon & Schuster Books for Young Readers. 1993.

Palmer, P. I Wish I Could Hold Your Hand . . . a Child's Guide to Grief and Loss. San Luis Obispo, CA: Impact Publishers. 1994.

Wood, A., and D. The Tickleoctopus. New York: Harcourt, Brace, & Company. 1994